GREAT CAREERS IN
SCIENCE

by Meg Gaertner

FOCUS
READERS®

NAVIGATOR

WWW.FOCUSREADERS.COM

Focus Readers is distributed by North Star Editions:
sales@northstareditions.com | 888-417-0195

Produced for Focus Readers by Red Line Editorial.

Photographs ©: Shutterstock Images, cover, 1, 4–5, 8–9, 11, 13, 14–15, 17, 19, 22–23, 25, 26–27; Mark Lennihan/AP Images, 21; Red Line Editorial, 29

Library of Congress Cataloging-in-Publication Data
Names: Gaertner, Meg, author.
Title: Great careers in science / by Meg Gaertner.
Description: Lake Elmo, MN : Focus Readers, [2022] | Series: Great careers | Includes index. | Audience: Grades 4-6
Identifiers: LCCN 2021009762 (print) | LCCN 2021009763 (ebook) | ISBN 9781644938478 (hardcover) | ISBN 9781644938935 (paperback) | ISBN 9781644939390 (ebook) | ISBN 9781644939819 (pdf)
Subjects: LCSH: Science--Vocational guidance--Juvenile literature.
Classification: LCC Q147 .G34 2022 (print) | LCC Q147 (ebook) | DDC 502.3--dc23
LC record available at https://lccn.loc.gov/2021009762
LC ebook record available at https://lccn.loc.gov/2021009763

Printed in the United States of America
Mankato, MN
082021

ABOUT THE AUTHOR

Meg Gaertner is a children's book writer and editor. She loves learning about advances made in science, medicine, and engineering. When not writing, editing, or learning, she can be found swing dancing or hiking the forests of Minnesota.

TABLE OF CONTENTS

CHAPTER 1

BRANCHES OF SCIENCE

Science is the study of the natural and social world. People often imagine scientists working in labs. But scientists work in a variety of locations. They study many different things.

There are three main branches of science. Physical sciences study the nonliving universe. Life sciences study

Some scientists work in labs, but others work outside.

living things. Social sciences study people and their behaviors.

Science is also a process. Scientists take what is known about a subject. They form an idea about it. Then they test the idea. They might do experiments. They might collect data. Scientists see

FORMAL AND APPLIED SCIENCES

Science includes two other branches of study. The formal sciences include math and computer science. The applied sciences take the knowledge of other sciences. They use it to solve problems. Engineering is an applied science. Medicine is, too. For example, medicine uses biology and chemistry. It treats health problems.

if the data supports their idea. If it does not, scientists change their idea. They continue their research.

Sometimes the data does support an idea. If so, scientists make sure their methods were correct. They make sure the data is **reliable**. Then they share their findings with others.

MANY SCIENCES

PHYSICAL SCIENCES	LIFE SCIENCES	SOCIAL SCIENCES
Chemistry	Zoology	Sociology
Physics	Botany	Anthropology
Astronomy	Molecular Biology	Psychology
Cosmology	Cell Biology	Economics
Geology	Ecology	Political Science
Hydrology	Genetics	
Paleontology		
Meteorology		

CHAPTER 2

PHYSICAL SCIENCE

Physical science includes four main fields of study. Chemistry is the study of matter, its properties, and how it changes. Scientists use this knowledge. Some chemists change raw **materials** into something new. The new materials might be stronger or lighter. Or they could be better for the environment.

Some chemists perform tests to create new materials.

People build products with the new materials. Some chemists focus on cleaning our planet. They detect pollution in the air, water, and soil. Other chemists make drugs for treating illness.

Physics is the study of matter, motion, and energy. Some physicists study the forces that cause objects to move or stay still. Others research light, sound, electricity, or heat.

Physicists have a big goal. They aim to discover a few laws that can explain how everything in the universe works. These are laws that all of nature must follow. Even the smallest and biggest things must obey these laws. So, physicists

Astronomers have sent huge telescopes into space to help study distant stars and galaxies.

study bits even smaller than **atoms**. And they study the motion of whole **galaxies**.

Astronomy is another physical science. This science studies objects in space. Scientists use telescopes and other tools. They collect data on objects that are far away. Some astronomers study how planets form. Others look at how stars interact. Some study how the universe began. And others search for life beyond Earth.

Lastly, the Earth sciences study Earth itself. Some scientists look at rocks and **minerals** in the ground. They study Earth's features. Others see how Earth has changed over time. They learn

TECHNICIAN JOBS

Scientists often need helpers for their research. Technicians fill these roles. These workers help run tests. They collect data. And they set up equipment. They also make sure the equipment works properly. Some technicians help solve crimes. They study materials found at crime scenes. Many technician jobs require less education than other science jobs.

A geologist may collect soil samples to look for evidence of pollution.

what Earth was like in the past. Some scientists focus on Earth's waters. They study the oceans. Or they look at the movement of fresh water. They work to improve the quality of water. Other scientists study the air surrounding Earth. They look at weather. They may study **climate change**. Or they may focus on forecasting big storms.

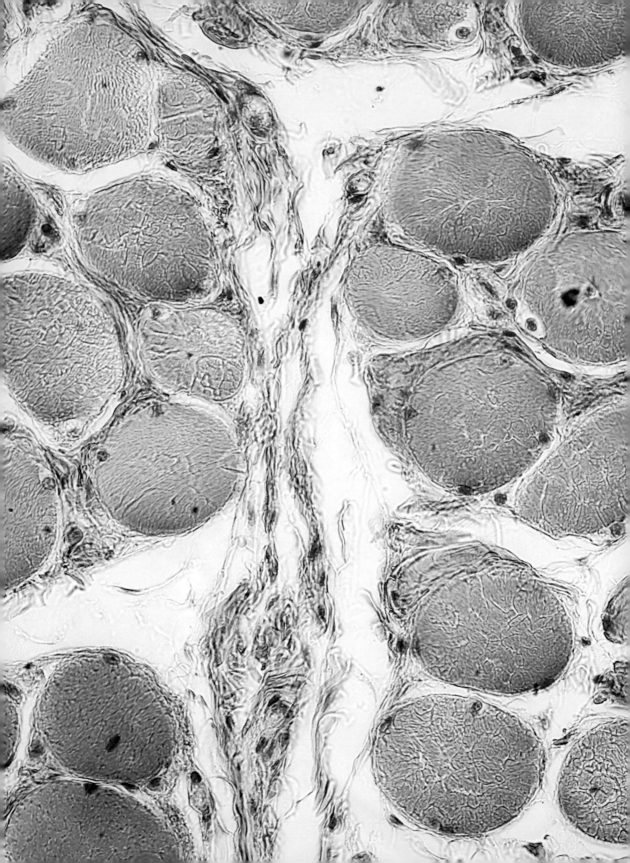

CHAPTER 3

LIFE SCIENCE

Life science is also known as biology. It is the study of living things and how they work. Scientists study life at different levels. Some look at the smallest units of life. These units are called cells. They make up every living thing. Medical scientists study human cells to improve health. They see how diseases affect

The human body has approximately 200 different types of cells.

cells. And they make treatments for those diseases.

Other scientists look at whole organisms. Organisms include plants and animals. Biologists study their features. They look at the different parts that form organisms. And they see how those parts work together to support life. Biologists also study how organisms behave. They often focus on one type of organism. One biologist might study the baobab tree in Africa. Another might study Bengal tigers in India.

Organisms also include tiny living things called microbes. People cannot see them without using a microscope.

Marine biologists study life in the sea.

Some microbes can cause diseases. Scientists study these microbes. They learn how to treat the diseases. Other microbes are helpful. Scientists use them to clean polluted areas. Some microbes even help crops grow.

Some biologists study **ecosystems**. They look at the relationships among different organisms. They see how plants and animals in an area interact. Over time, ecosystems reach a state of balance. Groups of organisms adapt to where they live. Different organisms keep others from taking over an area.

MOLECULAR BIOLOGY

Molecules are even smaller than cells. They are very important for life. For example, the DNA molecule carries a sort of code. That code is a set of instructions. It tells the body how to grow and survive. And it tells the body how to reproduce. Some biologists focus on molecules. They see how molecules make life happen.

Biologists may study rivers that have been polluted by human activity.

But sometimes, that balance can be broken. For example, human activities have affected many ecosystems. Large numbers of plants and animals are dying out. Some biologists focus on protecting these organisms. They work to keep plants and animals from going extinct.

VACCINE DEVELOPMENT

In 2020, COVID-19 spread quickly around the world. Millions of people died. COVID-19 is caused by a virus. Scientists have created a key tool for fighting viruses. It is called a vaccine.

A vaccine enters the human body. It trains the body to recognize the virus. The real virus might enter the body later on. If it does, the body will recognize it. The body will quickly fight off the virus before the person even feels sick.

Scientists worked hard to create COVID-19 vaccines. They performed many tests. They made sure the vaccines were safe and effective. Normally, vaccine creation takes years. But the first approved COVID-19 vaccine was ready in

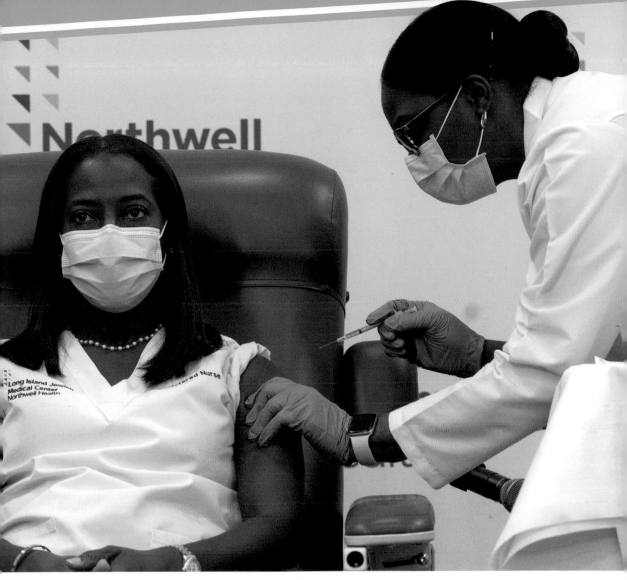

Vaccines for COVID-19 were first available in December 2020.

months. Scientists had been studying similar viruses for years. They shared their research with one another. Their work saved many lives.

CHAPTER 4

SOCIAL SCIENCE

There are five main social sciences. Psychology is the study of human behavior. Scientists study how people think, feel, and behave. They see why people do what they do. Psychology tends to focus on individuals.

Sociology focuses on people in society. Scientists see how being in different

Some psychologists study how children learn. That helps them create better teaching methods.

groups affects people's lives. Some scientists focus on social issues such as crime and poverty. They study the causes and effects of these issues.

Anthropology is the study of culture. Culture includes people's values and traditions. Some scientists study how cultures formed and changed over time. Other scientists compare how different people live today.

Economics looks at how goods and services are produced and spread. Some scientists study how people use their money. Or they study how buyers and sellers interact. Other scientists study the economies of countries.

An anthropologist may study ancient art and tools to learn about past cultures.

Finally, political science focuses on government. Scientists compare different forms of government. They see how different countries interact. Scientists might research the causes of war. Or they might see how countries can work together in peace.

CHAPTER 5

ENTERING THE FIELD

Some technician jobs require only two years of education after high school. People get associate's **degrees**. Then they are trained on the job. But becoming a scientist requires at least four years of higher education. People get bachelor's degrees. They study the type of science they are most interested in. Then they can

College classes help prepare students for careers in science.

get **entry-level** jobs. Beginning workers gain valuable experience. This experience helps them get better jobs later on. Many scientists also choose to earn advanced degrees. This extra education helps them get top research jobs.

Scientists need critical-thinking skills. They must think carefully about their research. This includes asking questions that can be tested. It also includes designing tests that will give reliable data. Scientists must be accurate when collecting data. And they must pay attention to details. Scientists also need writing skills. They write reports to explain their research.

Most importantly, scientists must be curious. They learn the answers to their questions by doing tests and making observations. Their findings often lead to more questions. So, scientists keep discovering. Science never stops.

CAREER PREP CHECKLIST

Interested in a career in science? As you move into middle school and high school, try these steps.

1 Take every science class you can. You will eventually choose one or two sciences to focus on. But it is helpful to have a broad understanding of all sciences.

2 Take math classes. Science involves collecting data. Math helps scientists understand that data.

3 Read books on the sciences you are interested in. Ask a librarian for help finding these books.

4 Tell your school's guidance counselor about your interest. This person can help you find opportunities to get experience in science.

5 See if your area has summer camps or after-school programs in science. Use the internet to find these opportunities.

6 Stay curious. Ask questions. Use the library and the internet to research the answers to your questions.

FOCUS ON
GREAT CAREERS IN SCIENCE

Write your answers on a separate piece of paper.

1. Write a paragraph describing the five main social sciences.

2. Which kind of science do you find most interesting? Why?

3. Which type of scientist works to understand the basic laws that guide how the universe works?

    A. chemist
    B. physicist
    C. sociologist

4. Which two scientists might work together to look at the way materials interact within living cells?

    A. an economist and a physicist
    B. an anthropologist and an astronomer
    C. a biologist and a chemist

Answer key on page 32.

GLOSSARY

atoms
The smallest building blocks of matter. They make up everything in the physical world.

climate change
A human-caused global crisis involving long-term changes in Earth's temperature and weather patterns.

degrees
Ranks given by colleges or universities after people complete programs of study.

ecosystems
Communities of living things and how they interact with their surrounding environments.

entry-level
Requiring no job experience.

galaxies
Systems of many stars.

materials
Matter from which things are made.

minerals
Substances that form naturally under the ground.

molecules
Groups of atoms that are joined together.

reliable
Trustworthy.

TO LEARN MORE

BOOKS

Carmichael, L. E. *Forensics in the Real World*. Minneapolis: Abdo Publishing, 2017.

Huddleston, Emma. *Studying Climate Change*. Minneapolis: Abdo Publishing, 2021.

Oxlade, Chris. *Dream Jobs in Science*. New York: Crabtree Publishing, 2017.

NOTE TO EDUCATORS

Visit **www.focusreaders.com** to find lesson plans, activities, links, and other resources related to this title.

INDEX

Answer Key: **1.** Answers will vary; **2.** Answers will vary; **3.** B; **4.** C